LIFE

Snacks

FOR
WOMEN

**CREATE A LIFE
OF EXCELLENCE**

**TIPS TO IGNITE
YOUR SPIRIT AND
INSPIRE YOUR LIFE**

Sharon A. Burst

SHARON A. BURSTEIN
—Award-Winning Marketing & PR Strategist

outskirts press

Testimonials - Life Snacks for Women - Sharon Burstein

"If you want to create a life of excellence with lasting impressions, you need to read Sharon's book, inspired and motivating. Her tips and strategies are life-changing ... it's a must read!"

Forbes Riley, *TV Host*
International Icon

"*Life Snacks For Women*, another brilliant book of inspiration, motivation and information by Sharon Burstein. These powerful little bite-sized tidbits are perfect for women of all ages navigating the world for every aspect of their life. A must read."

Lynette Louise, International Award-Winning
Speaker & Author
Brain and Behavior Expert
The Brain Broad

"An amazing book that makes you think! Sharon is a dynamic writer and speaker. You will be so inspired."

Kevin Harrington, CEO
Original "Shark Tank" Shark (ABC's TV Show – "Shark Tank")
Inventor of the Infomercial ($4 Billion in sales on TV)

"Sharon's books and powerful speaking focus on success and the positive aspects of life. She inspires and helps women center on what is truly important. Sharon provides ideas, lessons and simple reminders to absorb on a daily basis to be your best. An amazing book written for women in our time … right now!"

Marilyn Suey, Principal and CEO
The Diamond Group Wealth Advisors

"This fast-paced, enjoyable book shows you how to impress, persuade and influence people every time you "show up."

Brian Tracey, Legendary Speaker, Author, Trainer and Consultant
Top-Selling Author of 70 Books
Spoken for 5,000,000 people in US, Canada and 73 other countries

"When you open *Life Snacks* you are on your way to a life feast of your own road map to live your best life. The even better news is the fact that these delicacies are for every age and even invites shared reading out loud. Sharon Burstein bursts with lovely thoughts and words – all pouring for to make your life journey even more lovely."

Bob Danzig – Former President of Hearst Newspapers
Former Publisher Albany Times Union
Hall of Fame Speaker, Author

"Sharon is an amazing speaker, author and business leader. I love her book! If you're ready to achieve more success and happiness, then absorb the simple in this brilliant book by my friend Sharon Burstein! Her wisdom is life changing!"

James Malinchak, Featured on ABC's Hit TV Show
"Secret Millionaire"
Top-Selling Author, Millionaire Success Secrets
Founder, www.BigMoneySpeaker.com

"Sharon writes insightful books and is an amazing keynote speaker. Sharon's tips, stories and lessons are a must for anyone and everyone looking to develop and grow their Leadership Image and skill set."

Jill Lubin – 3 Time Best-Selling Author, Guerilla Publicity
International Speaker

"Sharon Burstein has the innate ability to present enlightening information that is full of wisdom. She has written a wonderful book that is educational, motivational and inspirational. Sharon is a dynamic writer, speaker and masterful leader. This is a *must read* for people of all ages who want to be more effective and achieve more in their personal and professional life."

Sharon Wolin, Principal – Sharon Wolin Productions
Television and Video Production

"An amazing book that makes you think! Sharon's a dynamic writer and speaker. You will be so inspired. This book provides individuals with tools to refocus while helping them and others to identify those areas where shifts need to occur in their lives."

Klio Demetriou, *Commercial Attaché*
Cyprus Embassy Trade Center, New York

Dedication

This book is dedicated to Roxanne Roth Blake and Susan Alpert Doninger Greer, two extraordinary women who have been a vital part of my life. I love you both, and the wonderful path and journey we have shared.

Table of Contents

Introduction
A Message to You

As women each of us is unique with none of us the same. We need to celebrate our significant accomplishments through-out life. Often we get caught up helping and inspiring others and forget to take time for ourselves. *Life Snacks for Women* words, tips and messages inspire and transform. They are healthy bite size tidbits and tasty morsels that you can snack on one at a time, or portion them out.

Life Snacks for Women is the second book in the Life Snacks book series. I wrote *Life Snacks for Women* to inspire women of all ages to look at life in a multitude of ways from different points of view. The words, tips and messages presented throughout the book were written to be uplifting, and make you pause, think, reflect and take action.

It's now your time to build wonderful you, to be the YOUnique woman and person that you are. Always remember that there is only one you and to yourself be true.

Discover and choose to be the amazing woman you are!

10 Point
Action Plan for Life

1. Demonstrate Your Happiness

2. Alter Your Mindset

3. Find Humor In Every Day

4. Find Your Strength

5. Have Gratitude

6. Persevere

7. Live Wisely

8. Impact Others – Change Lives

9. Become a Goal Achiever

10. Be YOU!

Accept

Accept who you are as a person and be accepting of others. Learn to listen and be open to other points of view.

As you go through life, remember that you do not need another person in your life to make you whole or complete. Strive to engage with people who are accepting of you. No one is perfect. Learn to accept and love the person you are, flaws and all.

Accept new challenges in your life and take action to turn them into success. It is through accepting and succeeding in life's challenges that you experience the sweetness of victory.

Teach your children and everyone around you to accept diversity. It is through our differences that we all learn from one another. If we accept only our own point of view and share our lives with clones of ourselves, we would be unable to understand the number of riches in our lives that we learn when we keep an open mind and heart.

Accomplish

If you have ambition, think you can and believe you can, chances are you will accomplish what you set out to achieve.

Begin your day with a list of things you want to accomplish in your personal and professional life. Start with a list of 3 things for each. Write them down each night before you go to bed. When you get up you will have your plan of action already in place so that you can begin your day productively and on the move.

Be the *Chief Encourager* and be an inspiration. People of all ages accomplish more when they feel encouraged. We cannot accomplish everything we need to do in our lives by working alone. Great things can be accomplished working together.

It truly is amazing how much you can accomplish when you know what you are doing, where you are going and how you are doing it. When you have clear and concise written goals you will achieve so much more and surpass others who never set goals.

Compliments and kind words do not cost any money, yet they accomplish so much.

Achieve

You gain great satisfaction when you achieve your goals, but even better is the person you become by doing so. When you achieve more, you grow more as a person.

When you achieve a goal, it puts a spring in your step, a smile on your lips and a laugh in your heart.

The road to success is filled with bumps and holes. It is how you react to them as you travel the road that determines what you ultimately achieve. Keep moving forward, sometimes you may need to slow down or stop for a moment, but never turn back. Commit to reaching your destination.

When you establish a strong capable team, you will be amazed at what you can achieve by working together.

Whatever your mind can dream and conceive you can achieve. To achieve your dreams and make them real the answer is simple, hard work. It is honestly that simple.

Affection

Expressions of affection, like holding hands, a light touch or arm around the shoulder, a gentle hug or welcome kiss, show you care.

Sometimes you need to invite affection into your life. Affection moves in two directions. You can give affection and receive affection. Having both adds greater balance to you and your life.

Give yourself a great big hug. You matter! Believe in who you are. Be in the moment. If you are all alone and in need of a hug, give yourself a self-hug, hug a pillow or something soft. You will find that it will make you more relaxed. This is a form of self-affection. Sometimes we women can all use an extra boost of affection.

Pets are great not only for the company and joy they provide, but for their calming affects and how both benefit from shared affection.

Authentic

Be authentic! Stand tall, express your thoughts and be authentic to the amazing woman you are.

Sometimes we fit into the mold of life around us, and sometimes you will find that it may no longer fit; that it is confining and you need to make changes in order to grow and be yourself. When you do, allow yourself to visualize who you are and the direction your path in life is leading you. Be authentic to the person you are today and the person you see moving forward tomorrow.

How do you become authentic and be the woman you want to be? First you need to believe in you, who you are and what you wish to do and be in life. One great step to help you focus is to create a list. Start with a simple list of 3 things and write them down. Create three titles and three lists: they can be on one piece of paper to keep them together. Titles could include: "I am …; 3 things I do well, and 3 things I want to do." Just be authentic in your responses. Keep the list in sight and read it everyday. As you accomplish each you will have a sense of great achievement. Keep making your lists and keep growing, but remain authentic to the amazing person you are.

We are all individuals, unique and real. Always strive to be the person you want to be in an authentic way.

Balance

Life has its ups and downs and some days life moves more in one direction than the other. The key is to develop greater balance and work to control the direction. While that is not always possible try. When you have balance in your life you will find that you have greater feelings of control and success.

Strike a balance and create realistic expectations for daily success. It is not how big a step you take each day toward your goal, but that you continue to move forward to success.

Having balance in your life sometimes means saying NO to things. Yes, it is ok to say no. Sometimes in life you need to say no to the good so that you can say yes to the great. While saying yes to everything feels good, so often as women we do not wish by nature to disappoint and want to be seen as team players.

While we all wish for superhero abilities, sometimes a few less demands and obligations add greater balance and allow you to be more effective and enjoy your personal and professional life.

Life is an exercise of balance, that is physical, emotional and psychological.

Be

Be all that you can be. Be YOUniquely YOU! Always strive to be your best. Be patient, be kind, and be generous. Be the person you are today, grow and be stronger for your tomorrows ahead.

No matter where you come from; where you are now, or what you have done in your life; you can always be a better version of yourself. It's not where you come from it's where you GROW from and what you choose to BE. Make a life choice and be the best YOU that you can possibly be.

Take time to be a great listener. You will always learn so much more by listening. Be in the moment and be open to all of life's possibilities. No matter where you are now, what you have and what you do, you can always grow and be better.

There is never an end to learning in life. The more you learn the more you grow. Be the best YOU that you can be and above all be yourself.

Cheers to amazing YOU, the person you are today and the person you are yet to be.

Beauty

The real beauty in a woman is in her heart and soul. Through life's passing years beauty grows within you. Be happy, laugh, smile and your days will be lighter and brighter. Believe in the beauty of your dreams.

Beauty is understanding and owning who you are and being happy inside and outside. It is being at peace with yourself and the world around you. Beauty is so much more than skin-deep. Beauty like your Leadership Image is inside, outside, top to bottom and all around. A truly beautiful person looks for the good in others and finds joy and joyful moments in every day. Beauty is looking beyond the surface. Each of us has our own style and individual beauty. The beauty of life is timeless and ageless.

There is so much beauty in the world. It is up to you to open up your mind and your senses to see it. Choose to be the person who inspires others.

You are amazing, you are wonderful, you are smart, and you are kind, you are significant, you are important, you are a gift! Each of these is a badge of your life, which is filled with bountiful and abundant beauty.

Believe

Believe in yourself and that all things in life are possible. You do not become what you want to be, you become what you believe you can be.

Women are much more powerful than they or you give and get credit for. Believe in you, go for the gold ring in life build visions and strive to reach your full potential.

Why believe in you? Simply put, if you do not believe in yourself why should anyone else? Learn to embrace and love the person you are. Believe in your values and what you stand for.

When you believe in something with your whole heart, you will be amazed how much of a force you can be, how strong you are and how much you can move and shift the direction and outcome.

Whatever you dream, imagine, ardently desire and sincerely believe, can take shape and become real when you create a plan, take action, keep moving forward step by step and believing.

Believe that you have value, bring value and are valuable. You are a treasure. Believe that you are YOUnique!

Blessed

Wake up, have fun, live each new day as if your life has just begun. You are truly blessed when you wake up, take a breath and start a new day.

We are all blessed when we have friends and or family that surround us who are there with both gentle and strong words that encourage and challenge us to be better in all aspects of our life.

You should feel blessed when you successfully accomplish a goal that you set for yourself and for taking the actions necessary that made it a reality. You made it happen, you visualized it and took action through to success.

Throughout your life there will be many people that you encounter that will provide nuggets and tidbits, large and small that will impact you and your life. What you take and absorb from them is largely up to you. When you see something in someone's life that you admire, it could be how they speak, act, dress, communicate, or a special way that they handle themselves as a few examples. Take those nuggets and tidbits and weave them into your life.

Look around you, feel blessed about the many diverse people you know and admire and give thanks to how they help you be a greater person.

Bold

When is the last time you felt bold in every part of your life in every way; your mind; body and soul? Be Bold, Be Brave, Be Wonderful Incredible YOU!

Sometimes we all need to be a bit bolder in our actions than we feel. There are times when you need to stand up and speak out! Find your voice and be bold.

Being bold doesn't always mean that you feel bold, but sometimes you need to express and be the person that is necessary in a situation in order to affect change and a positive outcome. Sometimes when you are bold you are being brave and that takes courage.

You can sit on the sidelines in life and help cheer others on, or you can choose to be bold, step up and play a more active role. Build steps that move you from the sidelines to the center of the action.

Breathe

Take time to breathe. Sometimes when life is hectic and you feel your life spinning, take a few minutes, stop and simply breathe. Breathe in and out slowly and work to clear your mind. Breathe in for a few moments and then exhale. It sounds simple, but this easy exercise will not only help you relax, but will help bring greater focus to your thoughts and ground you. Simple and effective!

Everyday that you wake up and breathe is a gift. So many things that you allow to build up inside of you can be let go. Breathe deep and blow those conflicts and troubles to the wind.

Before making a big announcement take time to breathe, pause and then make your statement. That one simple step will add greater impact to your words and message.

You breathe new energy into your life when you try new things. Think of yourself and your life as a sailboat. If there is no wind you do not go anywhere, but when the wind blows and you catch it in the sails the boat moves forward sometimes slow and steady and sometimes at gale force speed. The key is staying on track and not moving too far off your path or you will not reach your destination. Breathe and blow wind into your sails to move you where you choose to be.

Build

As you build your life, it is key to build a strong base that will support you through all situations and help you weather life's storms. The stronger your base and roots the higher you can move up and branch out as your strong base will support you.

Build yourself up to be around positive people. If you see elements that you would like to have in your life, weave them into your life tapestry. It will add greater depth and expand the person you are.

As you build your life make sure to have windows and doors that will help you to see clearly and ones that will welcome people inside.

Build your life with a solid foundation of values. As you live your life take time to remember and review your values and what you stand for. The foundation you build should be solid, but have flexibility and room for growth.

Calm

Sometimes you need to remain calm at least on the outside to others, even when that is not how you may feel on the inside. Calm is a state of mind and a state of being.

Just because you see that everything is calm around you does not mean that everything is still. Even when water or your life is calm, there is always movement above and below the surface.

When you are calm others around you will give greater notice to you than if you are loud and stressed. When you are calm it allows you to think more effectively and be proactive to situations rather than shouting, being stressed and being reactive. Keep calm and carry on is sometimes easier said than done, but is effective.

Be the person who is calm and the solid person that others turn to in difficult situations because they know that they can depend on you and your steadiness to organize and keep everyone together and on course.

When life starts to whirl around you and you are feeling out of control and need to calm you down, take a few minutes to breathe. Breathe deeply, hold it and release slowly. Step away for a moment if you can. When you take time to breathe it will calm you down, help your ability to think better and adapt to the situation at hand more effectively.

Challenge

It is when you challenge yourself that you grow the most. It may be uncomfortable along the path but that is part of your growth. How will you know how amazing you can be without challenging yourself?

Challenges can come in many forms. It is how you react and respond that will determine your level of success. The challenge at hand always begins with your mind, attitude and your belief in you.

Rise and face new challenges with firm commitment and belief of your success. Visualize your path through the challenge and set steps for your journey. You will achieve more if you take time to establish a plan of action and a timeline for success.

Change is a challenge for your future. We all face challenges large and small every day. Rise to the challenges you face, be bold, have courage in you and your ability to succeed.

Collaborate

Collaboration is about bringing people together and building success. Effective leaders know that when you create groups of people that have different talents and backgrounds and create an environment for collaboration, there is no limit for what can be achieved.

As women the more we can collaborate the greater our network in business and life. When you collaborate with others you build stronger opportunities for greater success.

Life doesn't always give you second chances. When you collaborate with someone you reduce your time and double your opportunity for success.

As you go through your chosen career, find or create groups of people that you can be mentored by and learn from, people who are further along their career path from where you presently are. Work to create mastermind groups that will bring you together in collaboration, and will encourage, challenge and applaud your ideas and goals.

Communicate

How effective are you as a communicator? Communication is a two way street moving in both directions. The art of great communication is becoming a master at listening.

How well you communicate and express yourself will affect the outcome. If you are clear about how you speak and verbalize your thoughts and ideas then there is greater clarity for everyone. After you communicate your thoughts and ideas, be open to questions to assure that everyone understands and has clarity on all points.

While there are times when we like to do things alone as individuals and not share what we are doing, you will find that when you open up and communicate your thoughts and ideas to others that you are able to accomplish more.

Compassion

Have compassion for others and have that same compassion for yourself. When you show compassion for others, you open up your heart.

Compassion brings together your mind and heart, creating greater understanding and goodness.

People cannot read your mind, but when you demonstratively show compassion you are communicating your feelings. Demonstrate your compassion for others and show that you genuinely care.

Compassion works in both directions. Show compassion to yourself and others. Compassion is something that we all universally need to give and receive.

Compliment

Compliments are like sunshine they brighten your day. Let's face it, we all love to receive them, so also practice giving them. Sometimes when you give someone even a simple compliment, you can visibly notice a new smile, or that they stand taller. Compliments can make a difference in your life and to everybody else's.

Find time every day to compliment others, whether they are people you know or simply people whose path you are crossing. Compliments make everyone feel great.

As a suggestion, practice giving at least 3 compliments to people throughout the day. Soon giving compliments will become a habit and a part of your day. Imagine if everyone practiced giving compliments how much kinder the world would be.

Compliments never grow old or tiresome. In many ways they are like receiving a giant verbal hug. They make you feel warm and good all over. Compliments make people smile and bring brightness to everyone's day.

Confidence

Confident women are both inspired and inspiring; they lift themselves up and others along with them. They shine in their success and on the success of others.

Have confidence in yourself and the person you are. Before others can believe in you, you have to be confident in you.

Confident women connect and build strong life long ties to other women who are successful in what they do. Build your mindset to be one that is brimming to the top with confidence. It takes courage to have confidence. Confident people have courage and courage builds confidence.

When you demonstrate and project to others that you are confident it will ooze like melting ice cream for all to see. Others will believe in you, and in what you are expressing and communicating.

To be an effective leader, you need confidence in yourself and with what you are expressing. Be confident in the person you are and what you believe in. Stand tall and project confidence.

Connect

As women, we need to do a better job of making genuine connections in our lives. The more you connect with people directly the stronger your relationships will be. Take time to create opportunities that bring you face-to-face with others.

While it is best to connect in person, social media and the telephone offer ways to always be in touch and connected.

Making new connections that develop into friendships is truly great. Sometimes these can happen as you connect with people while standing in line, someone you are sitting next to at a restaurant, and yes online. When you connect with others you open up and expand your life to new possibilities and opportunities.

Communicating by phone, and electronic or social media have their places, however there is nothing that is more effective than meeting someone in person, looking them in the eye, giving them a handshake, and a smile and having a great conversation together. That is when you truly connect.

Courage

Have courage in your life to believe in your dreams. Invest in yourself and have courage to take steps to move you forward.

Sometimes life can become difficult. There are times when you may wish to give in or give up, but that is when you need to dig deep within yourself and find the courage to move forward and persevere.

Courage is not about being happy every single day; it is when you are challenged that you find courage within. Courage is not about making the simple choice, or the popular choice, Courage is about making the right choice.

You will discover that courage is contagious. When you have confidence and courage others will follow.

Have courage, vision, wisdom and compassion in how you live your life. You'll never know how much change you can accomplish until you have the courage to take the first plunge.

Have the courage to listen to and follow your heart.

Discover

There is a wonderful world that is just outside of your doorstep waiting for you. Discover the limitless opportunities that it offers. It is up to you to explore the world and discover the countless joys that await you. Never feel limited in your life. Take steps each day to expand your world and discover new things.

When you dare to face your biggest obstacles you discover how capable and courageous you are. When you stretch yourself you grow. Dare to discover all that you are capable of being and how amazing of a person you are.

How will you know if you will like new things in life, if you never take time to try? You may discover that you enjoy different people, places, foods and things in life that you might not have thought possible. When you open yourself to experience and feel new things you will discover new things about yourself as well.

The only way you will find out all of your amazing talents is to allow yourself to experience diverse opportunities and discover things that bring you joy.

Dream

There is no limit to what you can dream. Dreams are visions for the future. Whatever you dream can become reality. Your dreams and visions today can be the realities of tomorrow. Think of your dreams as coming attractions yet to be released.

Dare to dream big. If you can dream it you can achieve it, but do prepare yourself to be comfortable with being uncomfortable. When you dream big you are stretching from where you are now to where you want to be. Your mindset is on the goal but your skill set has a gap that you need to learn, create or perhaps even invent in order for your dream to become a reality. The great news about your discomfort is that as you grow as a person you stretch your mind and imagination. Great dreams are worth achieving.

Everything began with a thought, an idea and a dream. Dreams and our subconscious provide our minds for what can be possible. It is up to you to give color, shape and texture to your dreams so that they take on dimension to become real.

Encourage

When you encourage someone be it a friend, family member, child, colleague or even a stranger, you are showing your support and belief in him or her as a person. Everyone needs encouragement through each and every stage of our lives.

Every time you encourage someone, you are inviting that person to take a step to achieve their goals, however large or small they be.

Encourage those you love and care about. Help them to grow and believe in themselves. When you encourage others, it helps to build their confidence and gives them courage to keep moving forward.

When you encourage someone you are demonstrating that you care and are showing your belief and support.

Faith

Have faith and believe in yourself as a person. We cannot see faith. It is intangible. Have faith and believe in your abilities.

As you begin to start up the ladder of life filled with vision and dreams you may not see the entire ladder, but as you take your first steps, have faith that you will be able to see more clearly with each step as you move up.

Have faith and believe in others. When you give them the right tools and express your belief and faith in them, you will find that they can achieve many great things.

When you are optimistic you have belief and faith in yourself.

Family

Find time to make time and spend it with family. Find the threads throughout your life that bring you together. Always try to keep three things close to your heart: your family; friends; and your integrity.

Family takes on many forms; there is your birth family, the family you grow up with, your family of friends, your work family, sorority or fraternity family, family of worship and many others. Every family is important in your life and is worthy of your love and respect.

Family is where life begins and love never ends. Even when we have our differences, which are inevitable, in the end family is there. Being a family is not just being together it is how you respond, support, love and are there to encourage one another that build a family, keeps them together and strong.

You cannot choose the family you are born into, however as you create your own family it is completely up to you how you design it and the type of parent and adult you choose to be.

Feminine

Embrace your feminine side. Learn to love the feminine side of you. You can be a successful and feminine at the same time, they are mutually exclusive. As a woman take time for you, even a few minutes each day. So often you can get caught up in life's drama that you forget to take time for yourself.

Our roles and the multiple hats that we wear each day as women can be many and varied. Take time to be more feminine and more lighthearted with yourself and with others.

There is a great deal more to being a woman than being feminine and the clothes you wear. We as women can dress and express ourselves in feminine ways while having a voice and a backbone that roars.

Through the past decades women have made tremendous strides in the business world. Our voices, talents and leadership are recognized and respected globally. We have developed greater confidence, that we can do anything we wish and if we can dream it, we can achieve it.

Be the woman with a voice who can roar and soar every day in every way!

Friends

The greatest treasures in life are friends. True friends are worth their weight in gold. A great friend is a person you can depend on; who is there for you during the good and more difficult times in life and is someone you can share your secrets, dreams and desires with.

A truly great friend is someone you may not see often or for many years, but when you reconnect it is like you were never apart.

Be the person that inspires and is there equally to laugh or cry and be there when help is needed. Be the friend that lifts people up, not kicks them down.

Great friends are honest and forgiving. A truly great friend will have you laughing when all you want to do is cry. A good friend is ageless and timeless.

It is wonderful to have friends from different areas of your life. They are like a wonderful bouquet with many colors, shapes and sizes.

Be a friend to you, believe in yourself. Listen to yourself and express your voice and thoughts as you do to your other friends.

Goals

You can create great visions and goals, but it is when you take action on your goals that your visions become reality.

As women, goals are always important for each of us throughout all stages of our lives. So often we get swept up in helping others with their goals that we neglect our own.

Throughout life your goals will change. Even if you accomplish all of the goals you set out to achieve, keep developing new ones, as you will never stop growing. The greater your dreams, the larger your goals and expectations for life.

Developing goals is creating a roadmap for your future and success. Your plan of action is your vehicle for how your reach your goals.

It all begins with your imagination, dreams, visions and then setting goals and a plan of action with accountability to develop them into reality.

Grace

Grace is about how you act and perform as a person and in different life situations. When you have grace, you are demonstrating control of a situation and not allowing the situation to control you.

Having grace can truly change and diffuse many tense life situations. Grace is a wonderful skill to develop, and combines mindset and attitude, both, which you are always in complete control of and never costs anything.

When you have grace, you are showing both elegance and eloquence.

Elegance and grace go hand in hand. Both have style and will assist you in handling yourself and others. Leaders have great grace and style; they always go the extra mile.

Have courage to stand up under pressure with grace.

Grateful

Find something to be grateful for every day. Being grateful does not cost you anything: it is being aware of your life and others and just simply for being alive.

Be grateful for the many wonderful opportunities that are part of your life. Sometimes you need to step back, take a breath, sit a beat and reflect on the many wonderful things both large and small that make meaningful differences and impact on your life.

Find a way every day to be mindful and grateful for what you have. At night before you go to sleep, think and reflect on 3 things that you were grateful for in your day. It will reinforce what you did and help clear your mind for a good night's rest.

There is no limit for what you can be grateful for. Every day is a true gift. We spend our lives racing all over and stressing on so many small things when we should stop, think and remember how much we are grateful for.

Humble

Words can be used to encourage and have the power to help, to build, heal, hurt, harm or humble. Take care that your words are used in positive ways. Once you express words verbally or in written form, they can never be taken back. It is better to be humble than harmful.

When you are humble you look beyond appearances from what the eye can see and the many blessings in your life.

Practice being more humble in life by showing greater compassion and caring of others and the world around you.

Humble people share the limelight, and credit, are team players and think not just of themselves but of others as well.

Be humble with who you are, but firm in your beliefs.

Humility

Humility is having a grateful heart. It is showing grace and being humble without being boastful.

When you have humility you are humble. Show others through your example that you care more for others than just yourself. It's not how you live, or what you do; humility is showing that you have compassion.

Regardless of how good you may be as a leader, a vital fundamental key is to have humility and to allow yourself to listen to others' thoughts, comments and feedback and learn from them.

When you thank people and express how grateful you are for their contributions, you are expressing gratitude and humility.

Humor

Find humor in something every day. A day without humor is a day wasted. Humor can bring so much joy and laughter to every day throughout the year. Face it, we can all use humor in our lives.

Humor is a great tool to use to reduce tense moments. In difficult situations, sometimes finding some light humor lessens tension and helps everyone refocus.

Humor is a great part of life regardless of age. Humor has no bounds and is universal.

Sometimes people use humor as a mask to hide or deflect their true feelings.

Independence

By definition independence, can be seen and expressed in many ways. It is a sense of freedom and the ability to be able to take care and be financially responsible for oneself. Throughout life we all go through different ways of both expressing and achieving independence.

Be proud of being independent, for standing on your own two feet, and for being responsible and embracing life.

Independence is the freedom to make your own decisions and to be self-sufficient.

Integrity

Integrity is doing the right thing, time after time, even when no one else is around. Having integrity is within you, a part of who you are and your center core.

Be honest with yourself and have integrity to stand up for both your beliefs as well as your mistakes. We all make mistakes, but it is when you accept that you are not perfect everyday in every way and have the integrity to show that and allow people see the person you are, that you and your integrity will shine.

Have integrity in all of your life's pursuits. Integrity is a tremendous trait to have and will always serve you well.

Integrity is making good choices that are moral and standing up for your beliefs.

Kind

Be the kind of person that people want to be around.

Being kind is a lovely virtue. Most times it is wonderful to be kind, but there are times when more of a backbone is needed. Life is not always soft, gentle or kind, but it is what we make of it.

When you are kind to others, others will be more trusting of you.

Being kind is an expression of understanding and compassion.

When someone does something nice for you, find 3 ways to thank them. You will feel good and they will feel tremendously appreciated that you took a moment in time to recognize their kindness.

Laugh

When you laugh, take a look at others expressions, as well as your own. See the smiles and joy that a good laugh can bring. Have you ever noticed how much better you feel after you have had a great laugh?

When you laugh it breaks tension and makes you feel good. When life is at its most tense, try to find something that will make you laugh, whether you are with someone else or by yourself. Even a quick laugh in a tense time helps to bring things into perspective.

It has long been said that laughter is the best medicine in life. Sustained laughter is great medicine, and a great abdominal workout.

The more you laugh the greater the joys you find in life. There are countless things to look at and laugh at... including yourself.

Lead

You can lead in life or you can follow: It is largely up to you. As you lead, learn to listen. Listen to others, listen to your head and with your heart and then make your decision.

Lead and be the leader that you are very capable of being. Everyone has the ability to lead themselves and others; the only thing that can ever stop you is yourself.

As you lead others remember to help build and bring everyone together as a team. When you lead, it is not about power, but empowering others.

When you are in the lead, people will always be looking at you. As you move further along or up the ladder to your chosen path of success, lead by example and always stay connected to others. Take responsibility as you lead to bring those behind you along and help them. You lead best when you are a mentor to others.

People think about leadership as a *position of power.*

Being a leader is about strength, courage, understanding, & sacrifice.

-Sharon Burstein

Learn

Be an ABLE person – **A**lways **B**e **L**earning **E**veryday. It's not how much you know it's how much you grow. The more you learn, the greater person you can be in your life. When you share what you know with others you learn more about them, and you help them build their knowledge.

Take a moment and consciously strive to learn something new every day. Be curious about everything around you. The more you learn about yourself, others, life and the world, the more curious you will become.

It is amazing to ponder that no matter how much you know and learn, that there is always more to learn. When you learn you gain knowledge.

You can always learn something from people around you. The key is uncovering the nuggets from others that can be woven into and add value to your life.

Often we do not understand what we need to learn until we learn it, and then see its value.

Love

Learn to love the person you are. When you love yourself you are more open to show love for others. Love is gentle, kind; it can be quiet, bold and does have power. Love builds and brings out emotion. Having love in your life is important, but love extends beyond you and people. You can also love places, things, a moment in time, your pets, nature and much more.

Love has no bounds. It is energy, a feeling. Giving love and receiving love makes you feel warm and cared about.

Sometimes a simple gesture, even a hand on a shoulder, a pat on the back or a simple hug can express love without ever saying a word.

You can feel love around you without ever hearing or expressing the word love.

Be the person everyone wants to be around and your home the place where people love to gather. We all like to be with people who are welcoming and embracing and places that feel safe and are filled with love.

Everyone deserves to have love in their life.

Mentor

We all need positive role models in every stage of our lives. The greater your success in life, the greater your responsibility as a mentor and leader to help bring the next generation forward to success.

So what are some of the reasons to have a mentor? Mentors inspire and cut your learning curve. They can assist you with your visions and putting your goals into action. Mentors can connect you to others and be a value to your life through the doors that they open. They are there for you to champion your success, keep you on track, hold you accountable, (sometimes we all need that boost or kick), and build your confidence. We all need assistance, connections, mentors and friends.

Find mentors you admire who have achieved success in areas you are building upon. Create ways to connect. Be a sponge absorbing all that you can. Having a great mentor will keep you on your toes and make you accountable for staying on track to achieving your own goals.

Mindful

Be aware of your surroundings and of the present. Be open and mindful of the vast world and countless opportunities. Stay mindful not mind full.

You have never lived this day in this moment before. Take a deep breath and savor the day and all that is possible. Be mindful that you will never have this day to enjoy again. Tomorrow it will be a memory.

You cannot make the perfect decision for yourself or others every day and in every situation no matter how mindful that you are. Even when you make a mistake, your mistakes are a way of showing others that you are trying, that you are listening and that you are mindful of the situation.

Think before taking action and ponder how you live your life. Be mindful of who you push away, what you throw away and what you do before you walk away. Hasty decisions are not always the best decisions. Think and evaluate your best options before taking action.

Motivate

The greatest person on earth to best motivate you is yourself. People can give you words and encouragement but it is when you take action and move your words into actions and deeds that you are demonstrating motivation.

As women, we naturally motivate and cheer others on with encouragement. While it is wonderful to be there to motivate others, always remember to give yourself a gentle and sometimes not-so-gentle nudge or kick to motivate you to your next success.

Motivation is external. Inspiration comes from within.

Think of yourself as a plant. The more you water, cultivate and care for a plant the more it will grow, thrive and bloom. The more you motivate yourself and others the same principle applies. We all need care to grow, thrive and bloom in life.

Each new day brings opportunity and new beginnings. You cannot reach the other side of the road unless you take your first steps. Only you can motivate yourself to take steps forward to where you want to go and how far you go.

Multitasking

Women by nature are born multitasker's. We are genetically equipped to perform a variety or different tasks at the same time. The key is not only to be great at multitasking but doing each task well.

When you find yourself in large multitasking mode keep a positive attitude. A suggestion is to stop for a minute and think about each of the tasks that you need to accomplish and create a plan. Why? You want to be successful, not wear yourself out. Plan and prioritize each task that needs to be done, with its own individual schedule and determine how it fits into your plan of action for the day. This one step can save aggravation, keep you in tune and in step.

When you do a variety of things simultaneously you are multitasking. Think of multitasking as juggling. You can have many balls in the air, but you still need to think and be in control. If you allow your mind to wander or add too many things for to long, some of the balls may drop and roll away with the others crashing around you. As you multitask through your day, be mindful of your priorities. Juggle a few things and work to complete a task or two before you pick up and take on more. It's not how many things you can do, it is about how much you can successfully accomplish with poise, grace and style.

Opportunity

Keep your eyes open for opportunities that present themselves for greater and more effective ways to communicate with your family and those around you. Sometimes opportunities jump out at you and sometimes they are more subtle.

When you know what you are looking for in different parts and paths of your life, you will learn to see opportunities. As you see them, seize them. Allow opportunities in your personal and professional life to propel you forward.

If you find that opportunity isn't knocking, build a door that you can open to get you to the opportunity that you are trying to reach.

You have the opportunity to be amazing. You have greatness within you, but it is largely up to you whether you seize opportunity when it presents itself or whether you let it pass idly by.

Optimistic

Learn to be optimistic. Being optimistic is all about your attitude and your mindset.

When you are openly optimistic around others you will find that people naturally respond to you in a more positive way and will look to you to assist them.

Be optimistic about your options and choices in your life. When you are open and have a positive mindset, you will find that you will see more and greater possibilities.

The more you surround yourself with people who are positive and are optimistic, the more you will find yourself and your attitude shifting the same way. Try to be positive in all situations, be open and optimistic of the outcome.

Passion

When you truly love what you are doing, you demonstrate your greatest passion.

Whatever task you take on, do it with passion, compassion and strive to do it with excellence.

Passion is part of life. There is nothing greater than feeling tremendous passion for things you truly enjoy. Be full of passion and passionate about your choices.

Sometimes you may find you outgrow your passions and need to move on and that is fine as long as you keep the fire of passion in your heart and life.

When you have a burning desire and the passion to affect change, how you act, coupled with your mindset and attitude will affect the outcome.

Prepare

When you plan and prepare, you significantly improve your opportunity for success. When you set goals, take time, think about your goal and write an action plan for each. These serve as your roadmap. Include a timeline for your plan and hold yourself accountable. Keep your action plan close at hand, and read and review it every week to check your accomplishments and keep you on track to success.

Learn from the past, and prepare for tomorrow by doing and being your best today.

When you prepare your mind and materials ahead of time for meetings and presentations, you will be more confident in yourself and project greater confidence to others.

YOU are a winner and were born to win, you have it in you, but you need to prepare, plan, believe in you and expect to win!

Pride

When you have pride it radiates from you. Take pride in both your accomplishments and the accomplishments of those you care about.

Women have tremendous pride. So often we are so full of pride about the accomplishments of others; including family, friends, children and colleagues that we neglect to have pride and celebrate our own accomplishments. Having pride is greater than an individual.

When you have pride it gives you a shining radiating glow. People will see it in your eyes, the way you walk, and how you present yourself.

Take pride and great care with everything you do. If you enjoy something, accept the responsibility, excel, own it and be full of pride.

Quality

Quality and excellence leave lasting impressions. Make sure the impression you leave on others is one of quality and integrity.

Quality or quantity? While you may be temped to have more, it is always better to choose quality, as it will last longer. While quality may come with a price, no one says you have to pay full price. Check out your options.

As you build your wardrobe especially for business, build it with a few classic styles that are quality and fit you well. Better fabrics also drape better on your body. Create your look and wardrobe for the position you want to have, not the position you have now. People will notice. Dress in styles that fit your body and body shape. Women come in all shapes, ages and sizes, one size and style does not fit all or any of us. Be you!

It's not the quantity of work you do, or the amount of time you spend, it is the quality of your work that makes the difference in every part of your life. The way you approach and do anything is the way you do everything.

Question

Have you ever been around a toddler and noticed how they are innately curious and question everything? The world seems to be one big question mark. When children are young we encourage them to explore their life and ask questions in order to learn. Keep that aura of wonder in your life and be inquisitive. It is through exploration and questions that we learn.

Learn to question and ask for clarity on things that you do not understand. Greater definition allows for greater understanding. When you ask questions you open doors to learning and life.

Imagine how many fewer things would have been discovered or invented if those before us had not asked questions. Let your questions flow like running water. The more you question, the more you learn. Raise your hand, sit in front, ask and question.

If you are building your career, looking to move in a new direction or start a business, learn to question and ask questions. Most likely there are others who have achieved what you are looking to do, be or create. Take advantage of their expertise and question them. You will learn so much, make great connections, and significantly cut your learning time. Learn to build connections with people who are above you that you can learn and grow from.

Realize

So often people go through their days and lives without realizing what they truly want to do. When you realize your goal, write it down and speak it, you are one step closer to making it a reality.

Realize that you have greatness within you. Dare to challenge yourself. Be the amazing person you are. Greatness comes from within. You have it in you to achieve greatness, but realize that the first steps to finding your greatness are up to you. Begin by taking small steps; as long as you are moving forward you are taking action. Keep moving forward; you will realize that the size of your steps increases as you build momentum.

Have compassion and realize that there are always a multitude of things to be grateful, and thankful for.

Release

As women, it is natural for us to gather and collect things. Sometimes we need to release some of our life's treasures in order to move forward.

When you are going through a tense time and need to calm yourself down, there is a very simple exercise you can do that has a great calming effect. You can do it alone or even in a crowed space and no one will ever notice. Using one or both hands at your side, move them slowly making figure 8's and breathe slowly. It is something you can do even if you are engaged in conversation. Be subtle, make figure 8's and you will feel tension begin to release.

Find positive ways to release your extra energy. You can walk, jog, swim, cook, garden... the list goes on. Channel extra energy in positive productive ways.

When you laugh it engages your body and releases your mind.

Relish

Bask, relish and savor the moment. Often during special moments we do not take time to look around, absorb and bask in the greatness of life's events.

Relish special occasions and moments. Take a snapshot in your mind and create a great photo memory. Think beyond the visual and absorb how the moment felt; the smells, tastes and sounds of the occasion. Create a memory file with all of the elements to be remembered and savored.

Some of the greatest moments in life are when they evolve naturally without planning. When those times occur; savor, relish and cherish the moment.

As a woman, you have an opportunity to leave a lasting mark and legacy to the world. Your triumphs are yours to make and yours to share. Enjoy the ride and relish life.

Resilience

When life hands you lemons, which it sometimes can and will, make a decision to make lemonade. Develop resilience and consciously look for ways to find the positive in whatever hand you are dealt. You cannot control the event, but how you respond to the situation will affect the outcome.

Your ability to be flexible in difficult situations shows others that you cannot be bullied and that you have resilience, will not be backed into a corner or allow unwanted situations to stick to you.

Persevere, take the best, get rid of he rest and move on. Show resilience.

Have great resilience and strength. When you are traveling a bumpy road, or headed down the rapids in a situation, focus on the positive, keep your eyes looking forward and your mind focused.

Mental resilience, a strong mind and determination will prevail.

Seize

The world is large and filled to the brim with opportunities. When you find an area you wish to explore, seize it.

When opportunity presents itself seize it, develop and cherish it as if you have been given a gift. The choice is yours as to what you do with it. Those who take action receive the rewards of their merits.

Seize forward with your eyes straight ahead and your mind on the end game. Know where you are headed before you arrive.

Carpe Diem! Seize the day, your life, hopes and dreams.

Smile

A smile can light up your day, and can light the hearts and minds or others. When you smile it is good for your heart, mind and soul.

Each day, find something that makes you smile. When you smile you open yourself up. Smiles are contagious; they open and inspire conversation and communication.

Have you ever noticed how when you smile at someone, they smile back? Imagine if we all smiled more how much happier we all would be.

Never ever underestimate the power of your smile. Your smile says a great deal about the person you are. When you see someone who is genuinely happy, you can see smiles all over their face, including their eyes.

Smiles and laughter have long been known to have many health benefits. What great medicine they are, with no cost and they help solve what ails you!

Give your smile a voice everyone can hear.

Strength

Strength can come from within and strength can come from being around people who love and believe in you.

Sometimes we all need to dig down deep to find our inner strength. It is always there, but sometimes the depths to find that needed strength can hurt. It is when you push through those times that you will find your greatest strength, soar to new levels and grow more as a person. True strength comes from within.

It takes strength to stand up to your beliefs with conviction. When you believe in something, it is up to you, how you adapt and whether you take any action. It is easy to let others take the lead, but when you stand up you build courage and inner strength. Your strength and action can have tremendous impact on the outcome.

Have strength. Believe in yourself and that all things are possible.

Success

Confident women believe that they are worthy of their success are proud of their accomplishments stand up and own their success.

Accessories make the difference when you dress. Think of your life filled with success and that you have a variety of successories.

Always remember that success is earned. You work hard for success, and put forth great strength, skills, sacrifice and time. Be proud of your successes. Give yourself a pat on the back and a great big self-hug. You deserve it!

Success is reaching your goal and then setting new goals. Always look for new ways to grow. Success is a journey with no two stories the same.

Always remember that success is a team sport!

Celebrate YOU and your success. Success like presents can be small or large. It is not the size of the success it is its relevance and significance for you. The only thing in the way of success is you.

Support

As you lead, learn how and when to support and be supportive. Both are equally important.

As women, it is important that we support one another and that we stand together, engage and learn from one another.

Sometimes your point of view may not be the same as others, but it is necessary to strike a balance and support the decision that is made.

Stand up and support things that you believe in.

Thank

No matter where you are or what you do, take time to thank people who make a difference. You can never thank someone enough when they have done something nice for you. Thanks can be expressed through words, actions, notes, or a gift.

As women, we are accustomed to thanking others. Recognize and give thanks to yourself for all that you do for others. It's not that you ask for thanks for the things you do, usually it's simply a natural part of who you are.

Look around and be aware of your surroundings and all of the natural beauty in the world. Often we trample through places and surroundings that we should be in utter awe of. Open your eyes, think about and thank the universe for the glorious world that surrounds us.

Practice writing handwritten notes of thanks, appreciation and gratitude. Everyone loves to receive a special handwritten note. They show that you took personal time and care to send a message.

Understanding

Take time and listen to different points of view with an open mind. Try to understand and be understanding.

Understanding is a major component in life. We cannot always have our own way and must be open to learning and listening to others thoughts, positions and views.

When you take time to understand with your eyes, ears, senses, sensibilities and heart, it shows yourself and others that all things in life are possible. Listen, Learn… Understand!

Be bold, be brave, be accepting, be understanding, be… You!

Understanding requires listening to and beyond the words being spoken to truly understand what is being said. Look at the whole picture before judging others. Listen to what is being said with an open mind.

Value

Your time has true value. Never underestimate that. Time is something you can never get back. Always remember the precious value of your time, and not to waste it.

Being a volunteer is a wonderful thing to do regardless of the role you play, the organization, or how much time you give. Through your kindness and generosity you provide enormous value to others to make a difference.

The value of trust is better and stronger than any currency. Trust takes a long time to build, but can be snapped and broken like a twig. Give enormous value to the relationships you build in every aspect and stage of your life.

Visible

Be visible, see yourself and allow your true self to be seen by others.

Often we assume that people know we are there for them and think that people will remember you and call upon you for projects, situations or leadership roles. What we think and what others think can be very different. You need to be visible to others in order for them to realize you are there. Remember; out of sight out of mind. Stay relative and relevant.

When you set goals, they become visible and take shape as you move them through action steps to become real.

Chose to be decisive and visible to everyone around you. Stand up, be heard, and be seen.

The pen and the writing of words bring the invisible to visible for all to see.

Vision

Dream that all things are possible. Having vision for your life extends well beyond goals. Vision is dreams for your future and looking beyond your present. There is no limit to your vision.

Even those who cannot see can have vision. Sometimes people who have sight have no vision.

Vision goes beyond seeing, it is looking beyond the horizon at what is possible and may not yet even exist.

As you look at situations, you can either look at each segment individually or take a broader expansive approach. Think with clear vision looking at the entire picture, rather than a glimpse or microscopic view.

Warmth

Warmth is much more than covering up, turning up the heat or making a fire. When you exude warmth, people can genuinely feel it without your ever expressing a word.

Show warmth and caring to others in the same way and manner that you wish it shown to you.

A genuine smile is filled with warmth and can be enjoyed universally.

When you are kind to others, you give warmth and sunshine regardless of the weather.

Welcoming

Open your door and heart and be welcoming to others. It is a very large world filled with people from diverse areas, states, countries, cultures and ages. Choose to be the home that is the welcoming place that everyone wants to visit and return to time after time, year after year.

When you open your eyes each morning, give thanks and gratitude for today and your tomorrows ahead. Be welcoming of opportunities that present themselves and open to expanding your mind and point of view. Be welcoming of each new day. Each one is a treasure.

Be you! Choose to be accepting, understanding and welcoming of the person you are.

Leadership and Leadership Image

1. Leadership and Leadership Image; separately they are great when effectively connected there is an energy that is unstoppable.

2. When you create an environment of openness and collaboration you open the universe and its energy for extraordinary possibilities.

3. Leadership is about building teamwork and trust.

4. If you want to be around great people you need to be open to ideas.

5. Enter the room as a sponge and soak it in. Be open, absorb and listen.

6. When you are with great leaders it is a privilege. Learn from them and adapt.

7. Give of yourself to mentor and raise others to new heights.

8. Life and Leadership is about connection and is energy chang-
    ing. Together they change the culture of your networks.

9. When you connect people together you create the capacity
    for change.

10. Leadership and Your Leadership Image are greater than you.

Powerful Women Word Phrases

Life Long Friends

Love You More

Nevertheless, She Persisted

Lead with Grace

Clarity of Purpose

Carpe Diem! Seize the Day!

Trust Yourself

Breathe and be Mindful

Life Snacks for Women

Special thanks and gratitude to the women listed below for their suggestions and ideas for words and phrases.

Roxanne Blake
Georgiana Becker
Ashley Becker
Brenda Beiser
Michele Bernier
Alexandra Burstein
Gina Marie Cannistraro
Brenda Cardenas
Carol Martin Carney
Sue Crum
Wendy Dahl
Susan Darrin
Violette DeAyala
Sherrie De Larm
Susan Ryan Dickey
Megan Faust
Loretta Fontaine
Lindsey Frick
Karen Gladu
Susan Doninger Greer
Lynn Hanley
Maggie Holbreiter
Amy Jordan
Dale L'Ecuyer
Karen Lane
Lynette Louise

Karen Peter
Colleen B. Macaulay
Sue Mandell
Sarah Martinez
Andrea Rogers McDonald
Maya McNulty
Grace Meaney
Kathy Miller
Mary Frances Millet
Connie Nadas
Melissa O'Reilly
Dottie Piroha
Alissa Quinn
Kim Saheim
Patti Silipigno
Sue Smith
Ina Soh
Marilyn Suey
Rhonda Sullivan
Susan Ungerman
Wauneata Waller
Deborah Willig
Heather Willig
Sharon Wolin
Kathy Yanas
Kimberly Zalankas

> **"To be successful, you need to feel successful."**
> **Sharon A. Burstein**

About
Sharon A. Burstein

Sharon Burstein is highly successful and one of America's most respected speakers. An owner of several businesses, sought out speaker, author, trainer, parent and educator, she has made meaningful differences in hundred's of thousands of peoples' lives. Sharon inspires people of all ages, building their Leadership Image and confidence to achieve more success in life. For more than twenty-five years Sharon has worked globally inspiring diverse industries, associations, universities and businesses. She has received numerous awards for her career achievements and leadership.

The roots of Sharon's career began in education, where she had the privilege of working with elementary age students as well as the collegiate level. Throughout her career, she has been a consultant, writer and sought out speaker. She later expanded her career in executive management working with diverse corporations and educational institutions before creating her own global companies. Sharon is highly respected in professional development and Leadership Image building. She is inspirational and motivational in all of life's pursuits.

Sharon has authored numerous articles spanning diverse subjects and the award winning books *Life Snacks – 50 Tasty Motivational Messages and What's Your Leadership Image.*

Contact: Sharon A. Burstein
Email: Sharon@SharonBurstein.com

3 Key Reasons Meeting and Event Planners Book Sharon Burstein

1. Dynamic Experienced Speaker

Sharon has worked for more than 25 years building Leadership Images spanning diverse age ranges, and backgrounds. She is a recognized award-winning leader has planned and successfully orchestrated hundreds of global events. Each speech and seminar is woven together with passion, humor and enthusiasm laced with entertaining stories.

2. Successful Entrepreneur and Business Executive

Sharon has more than 25 years of life, business and executive management experience. She effectively connects with each audience resulting in many "aha" moments. Sharon has owned successful consulting, marketing communications, broadcast and apparel manufacturing businesses. Your audience will be captivated, motivated and empowered.

3. Life Changing Message

Sharon motivates people to get moving and inspires them to develop their Leadership Image and set simple effective strategies in motion for success in life. Because of her diverse background, she connects with attendees. Sharon is unique because of her real-world experience spanning all levels of management functions and leadership. Her delivery is captivating and her contents are life changing.

Special Thanks

Writing a book is never successfully accomplished or completed by just the author. Along the path and journey there are numerous people who encourage, and assist in so many diverse ways. Success is a team sport and the success of bringing this book from concept to print has been no exception. As always I want to thank my daughter Alexandra Burstein and my husband Richard for their encouragement, love, support and suggestions, along with John Becker, Sharon Wolin, Sue Smith, Susan Culver Darrin, Forbes Riley, Bob Danzig, Jack Canfield, Jeff Hoffman, Klio Demetriou, Jill Lubin, Julie Carrier, Patty Aubrey, Dorothy Olendorf, Brian Tracy, Violette DeAyala, Lynette Louise, Marilyn Suey, Sandy Haber, Karen Gladu, Leone Modestino, Pat Jones, Wendy Dahl, Sue Crum, Lila Larson, Melissa O'Reilly, Maya McNulty, Sarah Martinez and Laura Stewart. My sincere thanks and gratitude to the many people who have inspired my life and its wonderful path and journey.

Printed in the USA
CPSIA information can be obtained
at www.ICGtesting.com
CBHW070520070424
6417CB00003B/4